I AM
HATZEGOPTERYX

by Timothy J. Bradley

I am *Hatzegopteryx.*

I can hatch.

I am *Hatzegopteryx*.

I can flap.

I am *Hatzegopteryx*.

I can leap.

I am *Hatzegopteryx*.

I can swoop.

I am *Hatzegopteryx*.

I can dodge.

I am *Hatzegopteryx.*

I can chase.

I am *Hatzegopteryx*.

I can gulp.

I am *Hatzegopteryx*.

I can grow.

I am *Hatzegopteryx*.

I can soar.

I am *Hatzegopteryx*.

I can grab.

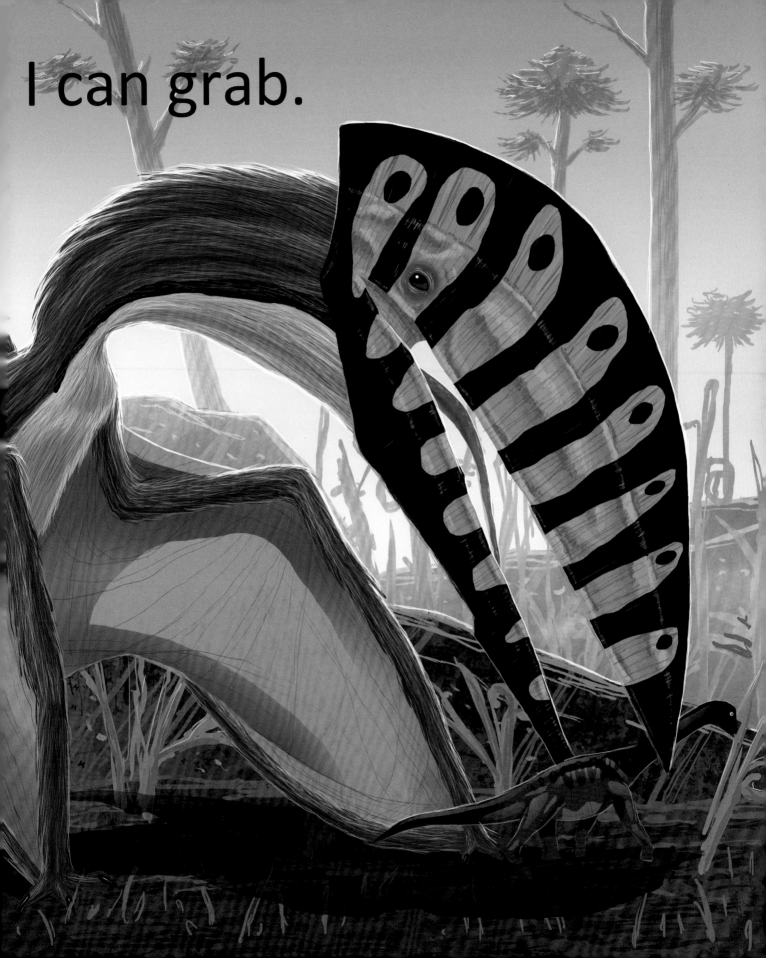

I am *Hatzegopteryx*.

I can gulp.

I am *Hatzegopteryx*.

I can leap.

I am *Hatzegopteryx*.

I am extinct.

For Creative Minds

Hatzegopteryx

The *Hatzegopteryx* was not a dinosaur but was a type of flying reptile called a pterosaur (TER-oh-sore). It lived about 66 million years ago during the Late Cretaceous Period.

Triassic Period (251-199 million years ago)	Jurassic Period (199-145 million years ago)	Cretaceous Period (145-65 million years ago)

Hatzegopteryx 66 million years ago

Hatzegopteryx was found in an area of present-day Romania called Haţeg (HAT-zeg) Island. During the Cretaceous Period, this area was mostly under an ancient ocean, with the area of Haţeg Island rising above the water.

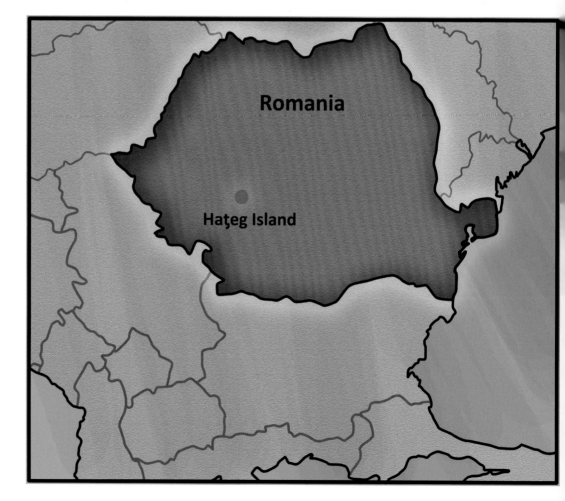

Hatzegopteryx versus *Quetzalcoatlus*

The *Hatzegopteryx* and the other giant pterosaur, *Quetzalcoatlus*, were the top two biggest flying reptiles ever. Standing, they were both about the heights of today's giraffe. The *Hatzegopteryx* had a shorter neck and a stouter beak than *Quetzalcoatlus*.

Paleontologists believe that *Hatzegopteryx* hunted on land. Its wings would have been folded into a walking posture, allowing it to search the landscape for small dinosaurs (just about your size!) to gulp down in one swallow. The *Quetzalcoatlus* also hunted on land, but ate smaller dinosaurs and reptiles

Quetzalcoatlus   Human   Giraffe

Hatzegopteryx

Head Crests

Like many other pterosaurs, the *Hatzegopteryx* had a large crest on its head that ran from the back of its skull all the way to the end of its beak. The pterosaurs had crests that were all different shapes.

Scientists aren't sure why they had such decorative adaptations. The crests may have acted like the rudders on an airplane, helping the pterosaur fly more efficiently. It's also possible that they were brightly colored and used to attract a mate. Maybe they helped the pterosaur to warm up more quickly, soaking up the sunshine. We may never know.

Whatever the reason, the flamboyant head crests of *Hatzegopteryx* and other pterosaurs made them very unique and fascinating prehistoric creatures.

Can you think of any animals that have head crests today?

Tupandactylus

Nyctasurus

Ornithocheirus

Dsungaripterus

Thalassodromeus

Today's Animals

Wings

There are many animals in the world today that can fly or glide through the air. Birds, along with some lizards, aquatic creatures, and mammals can guide themselves through the air. Flying or gliding is a great way to escape from predators or to hunt for food.

There are many different adaptations that allow creatures to move through the air. Pterosaurs had "hands" modified into wings—similar to today's birds and bats. If you look at the bones of birds' forelimbs, you can see that they have lost their individual fingers and have grown feathers. Bats' fingers have elongated, except for their "thumb," and have skin stretched between the fingers, making their wings. Pterosaurs had three very short clawed "fingers" and a drastically elongated fourth "finger." A layer of skin stretched from the end of the long fourth digit to the pterosaur's thigh.

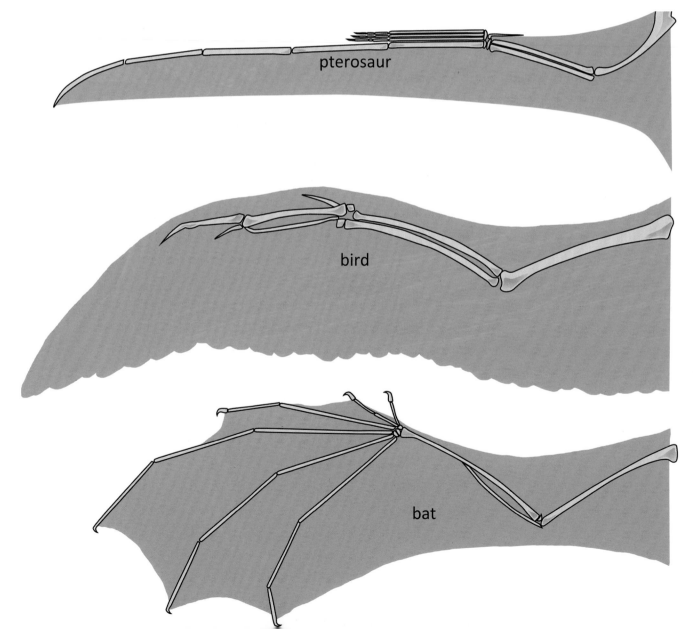

Library of Congress Cataloging-in-Publication Data

Names: Bradley, Timothy J., author.
Title: I am hatzegopteryx / Timothy J. Bradley.
Description: Mt. Pleasant,SC : Arbordale Publishing, LLC, [2021] | Includes
   bibliographical references.
Identifiers: LCCN 2021013699 (print) | LCCN 2021013700 (ebook) | ISBN
   9781643518213 (paperback) | ISBN 9781643518350 (adobe pdf) | ISBN
   9781643518497 (epub) | ISBN 9781643518633
Subjects: LCSH: Dinosaurs--Flight--Juvenile literature.
Classification: LCC QE861.6.F45 B73 2021 (print) | LCC QE861.6.F45
   (ebook) | DDC 567.918--dc23
LC record available at https://lccn.loc.gov/2021013699
LC ebook record available at https://lccn.loc.gov/2021013700

Bibliography

Fritts, Rachel. Hatzegopteryx, Transylvania's dinosaur hunter. Earth Archives. Internet. March 2020
Naish D, Witton MP. 2017. Neck biomechanics indicate that giant Transylvanian azhdarchid pterosaurs were
   short-necked arch predators. PeerJ 5:e2908 https://doi.org/10.7717/peerj.2908

Lexile Level: BR240L

Copyright 2021 © by Timothy J. Bradley

Printed in the US
This product conforms to CPSIA 2008
First Printing

Arbordale Publishing
Mt. Pleasant, SC 29464
www.ArbordalePublishing.com